THE LITTLE
BLACK BOOK OF

WINE

• *A Simple Guide to the World of Wine* •

ELIZABETH POYET

ILLUSTRATED BY KERREN BARBAS

PETER PAUPER PRESS, INC.
WHITE PLAINS, NEW YORK

THANKS TO SARAH POYET FOR
VALUED ASSISTANCE IN RESEARCHING AND
DRAFTING PORTIONS OF THE TEXT

*The Publisher wishes to give special thanks to John D. Bagdade
of Domaine Meriwether Wines, Eugene, Oregon
(www.meriwetherwines.com)
for sharing his expertise on the subject of wine.*

Designed by Heather Zschock

Illustrations copyright © 2004 Kerren Barbas

Copyright © 2004
Peter Pauper Press, Inc.
202 Mamaroneck Avenue
White Plains, NY 10601
All rights reserved
ISBN 0-88088-572-6
Printed in Hong Kong
7 6 5 4 3 2 1

CONTENTS

introduction

INTRODUCTION

Too often, the simple act of buying wine in a store or restaurant becomes unnecessarily complex and just plain daunting for the average wine drinker.

Knowing which wines to buy or drink with dinner can be equally as hard as pronouncing their names. Most of the time, we rely on the experts—wine shop personnel, wait staff, and sommeliers—and find the courage to ask for direction: "What's a nice red for around $20?" or "What do you recommend with filet mignon?"

We bluff our way through wine tasting rituals, nodding our heads with authority about a wine's quality or flavor, but not really knowing what, exactly, we should be looking for when we taste, and how, specifically, to do it.

Let *The Little Black Book of Wine* be your tour guide through wine country and beyond. Consider this book a short course on wine—minus the pretense, absent the arrogance—and learn the very things you need to know about what wine is, where it comes from, and how to evaluate it.

the low down on vino

THE LOW DOWN
ON VINO

Wine connoisseurs make drinking wine seem so complicated. With the grace and aplomb of orchestra maestros, they hold out their arms and swirl the wine in their glasses, evaluating subtle nuances in a wine's color that give clues to its variety, region, and age. They unselfconsciously stick their noses deep into their glasses and sniff, inhaling aromas that give them further clues about the grapes used to make the wine, the land upon which they were grown, and the manner in which they were fermented. And when at last they taste the

wine, they speak in a language all their own to describe a wine's "depth" and "nose," using terms like "long" and "earthy."

On the most basic level, however, enjoying wine relies on one factor alone—whether or not it tastes good to you.

And since taste is subjective, you alone determine the "quality" of a wine by evaluating the flavors as you imbibe and deciding, or not, to take another sip. Just as you may prefer aged cheddar to American cheese, or milk chocolate to special dark, the taste of a "fine" Cabernet Sauvignon may not be fine to you when it's a young, inexpensive Merlot that suits your tastes.

BASIC WINE TERMS YOU SHOULD KNOW

The first step to understanding wine is learning how to speak the language. The following description of key terms will introduce you to winespeak and get you started talking like a pro.

ACIDITY: Essential component in wine made mostly of tartaric acid naturally found in grapes. Low acid wines will be "smooth" and "round," but with too little acid, a wine can taste flat and dull. High acid wines feel "crisp" and "vivacious," but too much acidity can make them sour and unpleasant.

ALCOHOL: A colorless liquid by-product of the fermentation process that contributes to a wine's body and overall flavor. The alcohol level for most red wines falls between 11 and 14 percent, and for white wines, between 9 and 14 percent.

APPELLATION: The official name of the geographic location for growing grapes, usually found on a wine's label, and often part of its name.

AROMA: The individual smells or flavors of a wine that include, among other categories, fruits, spices, flowers, and earth.

BALANCE: The combination of acidity, sweetness, tannins, and alcohol in a wine. Quality wines are well-balanced, with no single component dominating another.

BODY: The impression of weight and size of a wine, usually described as light, medium, or full. Full-bodied wines feel bigger and heavier in the mouth.

BOUQUET: Refers to the multi-layered combination of smells or flavors in a wine.

COMPLEXITY: The depth (see below) of a wine, made of many different aromas and flavors.

DECANT: To transfer wine from a bottle into a container or glasses to allow it to aerate or breathe. Aerating younger wines may soften harsh flavors, while decanting older red wines allows for

sediment to be poured off and any unpleasant odors to be released.

DEPTH: The multi-dimensional flavors of a fine wine.

FERMENTATION: The natural process by which wild or cultured yeast transforms the sugars in grape juice to create alcohol, or wine.

FINISH: The aftertaste, or final impression, of a wine after it has been swallowed or spat.

LEES: Sediment composed of grape solids and yeast cells that forms at the bottom of a barrel or tank following fermentation.

LEGS: The dripping lines, or tears, wine forms after it has been swirled inside a glass. The more legs the wine has, the more viscous it is, often an indicator of higher alcohol content.

MOUTHFEEL: The texture of a wine as sensed by the mouth and tongue.

PALATE: The flavor or taste of a wine.

SOMMELIER: French name for a wine expert. In some restaurants, the sommelier assists customers with wine selection, presentation, and service.

TANNIN: Substance found in grape seeds and stems that serves as a natural preservative in wine. Tannin dries the mouth, leaving a puckery after-taste that lends a smooth, mellow flavor to aged wines or a rough, harsh taste to young red wines. When well matched by the other elements, tannin contributes to the backbone and structure of a good red wine. Cabernet Sauvignon and other full-flavored reds contain high amounts of tannins.

TASTEVIN: This word generally reserved for connoisseurs and sommeliers (literally, "taste wine") refers to the small silver cup first used for

tasting wine in underground wine cellars. The round depressions that decorate the cup reflected the candlelight, allowing the wine to be seen in near-darkness.

VARIETAL: Refers to the variety or type of grape used to make a wine.

VINTAGE: The year grapes were harvested to make a wine.

VISCOSITY: The body or thickness of a wine, usually used when discussing wines that have high sugar or alcohol content.

WINEMAKING AT A GLANCE

Understanding the basic process of winemaking—which has changed very little since wine was first made many centuries ago—plays an important role in recognizing and appreciating the flavors in the type of wines produced.

It takes an average of 2-1/2 pounds of grapes to create enough liquid to fill one wine bottle.

There are five main steps in wine-making:

- Harvesting the grapes (by hand or machine)
- Juicing the grapes (by machines that press or crush the grapes)
- Fermenting the grapes (occurs naturally when yeast feeds on sugar in grapes to form alcohol and carbon dioxide)
- Filtering the wine (removes sediment and "cleans" the wine)
- Bottling the wine (wine is transferred to clean, sterile bottles and aged weeks, months, or years)

Vinification, or winemaking, is truly an art in terms of the role individual winemakers play. They make hundreds of decisions regarding how grapes are grown and harvested, how they will be fermented (usually in oak barrels or stainless steel tanks) and, perhaps, blended, and how long they will be aged. Other factors, such as the geographic location of the vineyard, soil composition, and exposure to the elements (sun, wind, and water) all contribute to a wine's quality, flavors, and personality.

SUFFERING FROM SULFITES?

Sulfites occur naturally in wine as a result of fermentation, and are also added in small, regulated amounts to retard spoilage. A tiny proportion of the population, generally people with severe asthma, may have a reaction to these compounds, which are also present in many foods found on grocery shelves. For the vast majority of people, they are of no concern.

RED, PINK, AND WHITE

When most people discuss wine, they are usually referring to table wine—the common, non-carbonated wine served with or without food that contains less than 14% alcohol. Table wine can be red, pink, or white, determined entirely by the presence or absence of skins during the fermentation process (known as skin contact).

Red wines, such as Cabernet Sauvignon, Merlot, Pinot Noir, and Zinfandel, derive their deep, rich color from pigments in red grape skins called anthocyanins. Grape skins also contain tannin, a substance that imparts a dry, somewhat bitter flavor in red wines not found in white wines. The longer grape juice stays in contact with the skins, the more tannic the wine becomes.

The pink hues of rosé or blush wines

result when the juice of red grapes has fermented briefly with their skins. White wines such as Sauvignon Blanc, Chardonnay, Pinot

Grigio, and Riesling are produced when no skin contact takes place between the skins of green or red grapes and their juice.

Regardless of color, the amount of sugar and alcohol largely impact a wine's overall flavor. A wine tastes "dry" when all the original sugars in the grapes have been transformed into alcohol. Good examples include Merlot and Syrah for reds, as well as white Sauvignon Blanc and Chardonnay, which contain 12% to 14% alcohol. In a "sweet" wine, only part of these sugars has been converted to alcohol. With 3% residual sugar, for example, a wine will taste off-dry, or slightly sweet; a simple Riesling is a good example, with an alcohol level between 11% and 12%.

Fruity flavors are mostly found in young

wines. Two grape varieties with a propensity for fruitiness are Gamay, with its suggestion of black cherry, and Gewürztraminer, with its deep, fruity aroma. (Read more about flavors of specific grape varieties on pages 48-65.)

BUBBLY AND STRONG

Wine may also be divided into two other categories: sparkling and fortified.

SPARKLING WINES get their bubbles from the carbon dioxide naturally produced during fermentation. Whereas carbon dioxide is released from barrels, containers, or tanks while table wine develops, sparkling wines undergo a second fermentation in closed containers to capture these natural gases, and take on a fizzy, carbonated structure. Champagne, often made from Red Pinot

Noir, Pinot Meunier, or Chardonnay grapes, is perhaps the best known sparkling wine.

FORTIFIED WINES, also known as dessert, sweet, or liqueur wines, contain 5-30% sugar and more than 14% alcohol. Port and Sherry are two common fortified wines, all of which contain additional alcohol that is added either before or during fermentation.

These sweet wines are made in two ways. First, winemakers may leave the grapes on the vine longer while sugar levels continue to rise. The mold *botrytis* is allowed to thrive on some grapes, dehydrating them to further intensify their sweetness; Sauternes and Gewürztraminers are good examples. Alternatively, the grapes can be left unharvested until the water in them freezes; the sugar content is then extracted, to make so-called ice wine.

CHOOSING THE RIGHT BOTTLE

The key to wine shopping is to take it less seriously. Remember, no one can possibly know everything about wine because it's constantly changing; new wineries, vintages, and technology are just a few reasons why.

Be honest about what you know—and don't know—and approach your wine buying with a sense of fun and adventure. After all, it's just wine—a delicious, alcoholic, fruity beverage designed solely for our enjoyment.

Here are a few tips to help you make the most out of your wine shopping:

Read about wine and keep a list of recommended bottles and their price ranges. Good wine need not cost a fortune. In fact, you can find numerous enjoyable wines for about $10 per bottle. But since wine can cost anywhere from a few dollars to hundreds of dollars, it's important to decide how much you want to spend before you shop.

● Know what you like. Red, white, or sparkling? "Fruity" and "sweet"? Or "crisp" and "dry"?

● Don't be afraid to ask questions of wine sales staff. The most reliable sources of information are usually the wine retailers with personal knowledge of the wines they sell—as opposed to those who rely on the same magazine articles or critics' scores you've read for your information.

Be adventurous and experiment by trying out new wines from different corners of the world. You win some and you lose some, but the more wines you taste, the more knowledgeable you will become.

TO SERVE AND PRESERVE

When a bottle of wine makes it from its producer to your home, the manner in which you store it, serve it, and preserve it can greatly affect the way it tastes.

STORING WINE

If you buy wine by the case and keep the bottles only weeks or months, the most important factor is maintaining a temperature that never goes above 65°F (18°C). A small wine rack is handy for storing a small number of bottles horizontally, so that contact is always maintained between wine and cork.

Storing wine properly over a long period of time is a greater challenge. Bottles must be placed horizontally

in a dark room with good ventilation, free of vibrations. Temperature should remain a constant 50°-59°F (10°-15°C). Humidity must stay between 60% and 80% to prevent corks from drying out. A bowl of water in the storage area can help. A good solution can be a room on the north side of the house with its own thermostat, or a closet or cupboard under the staircase. If you have the money, the best solution is a specialized, temperature-controlled wine cabinet or a cellar dug into the ground.

THE RIGHT GLASS

Believe it or not, choosing the right glass in which to serve wine makes a difference in how the wine tastes.

Of course, wine glasses should be completely clean and free of dust to avoid contaminants. Harsh detergents can

compromise the taste of the wine, so wash glasses separately, preferably by hand, with warm water and a small amount of soap. Rinse the glass in hot water, but not too hot, as this could crack the glass. Drain the glass upside down, but plan to store it right side up, to protect the rim. Remove spots with a soft cloth if necessary.

The shape of a wine glass can also affect the taste of a wine and the ease with which to evaluate it. A good wine glass has a generous bowl, so that the wine may be swirled without risk of spilling, and the aromas and flavors can express themselves. It is narrower at the top, to focus the odors as you smell the wine, and its rim is thin, allowing the wine to slide past it smoothly.

Since red wines especially need to

breathe, the bowls of glasses for red wines are generally wider than for white wine glasses.

Cut crystal is lovely to behold, but prevents the taster from examining the wine properly. Choose a smooth, clear glass instead. Finally, the stem must be long enough so the glass may be held without touching and warming the bowl.

LETTING WINE BREATHE

The flavor of many wines, especially tannic reds, becomes more apparent and pleasurable when exposed to air. To do this effectively, the wine should be poured into a carafe so that it is exposed to sufficient amounts of oxygen. Decanting older red wines also serves to clear them of any sediment.

NOT TOO WARM, NOT TOO COLD

Red wines are generally served at room temperature, or 60°-65°F. If the room is warmer than this, and if the wines have not just been brought from a cellar, chill them very briefly to bring the temperature down. If the wine is too cold, it may taste bitter or tannic; served too warm, it can taste over-ripe.

The exception to the above rule is Beaujolais, which is generally chilled to enhance its fruity flavors. White wines are also served chilled, as that best displays their character.

PRESERVING AN OPENED BOTTLE

Wine begins to oxidize more rapidly once the bottle is opened, due to contact with the air. Re-stopping the bottle and placing it in the refrigerator slows oxidation somewhat. A more effective solution is to use a simple, inexpensive vacuum tool to pump the air out of the bottle before storage. Wine treated in this way can be kept about 48 hours.

developing your
wine sense

DEVELOPING YOUR WINE SENSE

The art of tasting a wine involves three basic steps that, in turn, involve the senses of sight, smell, and taste. And note:

● To clear the sensory palate, so to speak, do not wear perfume or lipstick while tasting wine, or expect to taste the wine accurately if there are other strong aromas in the room.

● When pouring the wine, be sure to fill the glass no more than halfway, so that the wine may be properly swirled and savored.

EYEING A GLASS

The visual appearance of a wine—the color, hue, and legs—indicates its body or weight and alcoholic strength.

Evaluate the color of the wine by holding up the glass at a 45° angle in front of a white background, such as a tablecloth. Remember that flavor is unrelated to color. But color is related to age: red wines get lighter as they age, while the opposite is true for whites.

Look for the different hues in each grape variety. Chardonnay is golden, compared to the pale, rather greenish yellow of Riesling. Gamay is cherry red, Pinot Noir is a slightly pale vermilion, Zinfandel is purplish, and Cabernet Sauvignon a bluish-black.

If the wine looks hazy or bubbly, this indicates problems have occurred during fermentation or filtration.

Swirl the wine around the inside of the glass. The dripping lines formed by the wine as it falls back down after swirling are called tears or legs. The more legs the wine has, the higher the alcohol content.

DESCRIBING A WINE'S APPEARANCE

- Brilliance
- Clarity
- Cloudiness
- Color
- Denseness
- Dullness
- Hue
- Legs
- Sediment

FOLLOWING YOUR NOSE

The "nose" of a wine is its smell. Assess aroma by swirling the wine again, then putting your nose into the glass and inhaling deeply or in several quick bursts. Inhaling with your mouth open a bit can help you smell. The nose soon tires, but comes back quickly; give your nose a rest and try again.

Flaws in the wine usually can be smelled immediately. Corked wine, for example, contains traces of 2-4-6 Trichloranisole (TCA), due to the presence of this bacterial product on the cork that resists sterilization. The resulting musty, unpleasant aroma and off flavor causes many bottles to be rejected at the restaurant table. The new screw-top bottle closure eliminates this problem. Oxidation yields a dull odor of sherry; excess sulfur lends an aroma of burnt matches.

Excess hydrogen sulfide leaves a smell of rotten eggs, removable by decanting, which adds air to the wine. Sometimes the wine has begun to turn to vinegar.

Here are some sample descriptive terms for verbalizing what you smell in your glass of wine. Keep in mind that these are not universal, as perception of aroma varies from person to person.

DESCRIBING A WINE'S AROMA

FRUITY: red fruits, such as cherry, raspberry, strawberry, plum; citrus fruits such as lemon and orange; tropical fruits such as mango and pineapple; pitted fruits such as peach or apricot.

SPICY: pepper, cedar, cinnamon, mint.

FLORAL: honeysuckle (whites); violet, rose (reds); geranium.

VEGETAL: cabbage, bell pepper (reds); olives; green or grassy, such as asparagus; garden pea (whites); green beans; earthy, such as mushrooms.

CHOCOLATE: mocha, milk chocolate.

SAVORY: coffee, beef, soy (reds).

MINERAL: pebbles, fresh soil, stony.

ANIMAL: sweat, barnyard.

DISCERNING TASTES

The taste of the wine, as we experience it, is actually composed of four elements: taste, aroma, body, and texture.

TASTE

The tongue is capable of registering four tastes: sweetness on its tip, sourness or acidity on the sides, and bitterness, such as tannin, at the back. (The fourth  taste, saltiness, is not normally found in wines.) Swishing the wine around in your mouth brings it into contact with all the tasting areas on the tongue.

AROMA

Up to 10,000 other flavors come not from the tongue but from the nasal receptors in the olfactory bulb. Air drawn through the wine into your mouth vaporizes the aromas, which float up to the receptors through the

retronasal passage. This is why neither food nor wine has much taste when you have a cold: the receptors are blocked and cannot function properly.

BODY

Body is the impression of the weight and size of wine. A wine with full body seems fuller, bigger, heavier in the mouth; it seems to coat your throat like cream. A light-bodied wine slips easily across the palate, like skim milk. A Chardonnay, for example, has fuller body than a Riesling.

TEXTURE

Mouthfeel is the textural impression of softness and smoothness, versus firmness, coarseness, or roughness in a wine. Fabric names are sometimes used to describe texture: smooth as silk, soft as flannel. High acidity in white wines yields hardness, firmness, crispness of texture; high tannin gives similar results in reds. Low levels of these components create softness, which can be excessive. Unfermented sugar and alcohol also yield softness, although very high alcohol content will give a hard edge.

SWISHING AND CHEWING

As soon as the tip of your tongue touches the wine, decide if it is sweet or dry. Next, consider acidity, the backbone of a white wine. Without sufficient acidity, white wines seem soft, fat, and flabby. With good acidity, whites are crisp or tart. Tannin provides a similar structure to red wines. A red with high tannin is described as astringent; medium tannin, firm; or low tannin, soft.

Consider what family of flavor the wine represents. Is it fruity, spicy, herbal? What specific aromas within the family can you identify? Is the wine light, medium, or full-bodied? Is it smooth or hard?

What is the quality of the wine? Does it have any flaws? Is it balanced? Is it too young, or past its prime?

WORDS USED TO DESCRIBE WINE

Acidic	Fruity
Approachable	Full-Bodied
Balanced	Herbal/
Big	Herbaceous
Bitter	Intense
Chewy	Light
Closed	Long (or short)
Cloying	Meaty
Coarse	Oaky
Complex	Rough
Crisp	Simple
Dry	Smooth
Elegant	Soft
Fat	Spicy
Faulty	Tannic
Flabby	Tart
Fleshy	Toasty

THE FINAL ANALYSIS

Wine leaves a distinct impression on the tongue and mouth after it has been swished, chewed, and swallowed.

BALANCE

The interrelationship of the four major components of a wine determines its balance: alcohol and sugar soften the wine; acidity and tannin give structure to the wine. The wine is balanced if none of the elements is too prominent.

LENGTH

This is one of the first indicators of high quality. Long describes a wine that you can taste fully during the first sip, all across your tongue, and it lingers at the back of your mouth. A short wine may start with a bang but lose its taste almost immediately.

COMPLEXITY

A complex wine offers many different impressions as you drink it. This is another sure sign of quality.

DESCRIPTORS FOR A GOOD WINE

- Concentrated (intensely flavorful)
- Crisp (pleasantly acidic)
- Firm (pleasantly tannic)
- Fresh (pleasantly acidic)
- Mature (sufficiently aged)
- Round (good body and not too tannic)

DESCRIPTORS FOR A BAD WINE

- Astringent or Hard (too tannic or bitter)
- Corked, Musty, or Off (moldy or spoiled)
- Flabby (not acidic enough)
- Green (unripe)
- Hollow or Lean (not fruity enough)
- Hot (too much alcohol)
- Tart (too acidic or sour)

the mighty grape

TYPES OF GRAPES

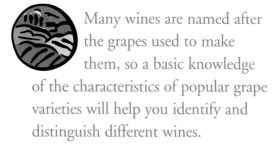 Many wines are named after the grapes used to make them, so a basic knowledge of the characteristics of popular grape varieties will help you identify and distinguish different wines.

MAIN WHITE VARIETIES

CHARDONNAY

TYPICAL STYLE: dry white

AROMAS: tropical fruit, pineapple, apple, lemon; oak from barrel fermentation

MOUTHFEEL: smooth, creamy, full-bodied

ACIDITY: medium

REGIONS: France (Burgundy, Chablis, Champagne, Languedoc-Roussillon, southern France), California, Washington,

Oregon, New York, Australia, New Zealand, South Africa

ACCOMPANIES: seafood, salmon, fish, poultry

The Chardonnay grape yields the greatest white wines in the world—the Burgundy whites, for example, such as Montrachet and Meursault and Chablis—and is an important component of champagne. Chardonnay has recently become one of the most successful whites internationally.

CHENIN BLANC

TYPICAL STYLE: ranges from bone-dry to off-dry/rather sweet

AROMAS: melon, nut, pear, apricot, peach, apple

MOUTHFEEL: crisp

ACIDITY: high

REGIONS: France (Loire Valley: appellations Vouvray, Savennières are superior), California, South Africa

ACCOMPANIES: appetizers, trout, sole and other white fish, chicken

This is not a very common wine in the U.S.

RIESLING

TYPICAL STYLE: dry to sweet
AROMAS: apple, citrus, peach
MOUTHFEEL: light
ACIDITY: very high
REGIONS: Germany, France (Alsace), Washington, Oregon, Idaho, California, New York, Australia, New Zealand
ACCOMPANIES: seafood, crab, smoked salmon and trout, fish, fatty birds (duck, goose), sauerkraut

The Riesling grape yields softer, fuller, fruitier wines with less natural acidity in warmer areas, but the most refined ones come from cooler climates. The best examples of this unique wine are

popular among connoisseurs. One reason it lacks popularity among non-experts is that many poor quality wines masquerade under the Riesling name. Many ice wines are made from this grape variety.

SAUVIGNON BLANC

TYPICAL STYLE: dry white

AROMAS: green fruit, grass, herbs, gooseberry, cat pee

MOUTHFEEL: crisp

ACIDITY: high

REGIONS: France (Loire Valley: Pouilly-Fumé, Sancerre; Bordeaux: Graves), New Zealand, Austria, South Africa, Washington, California, Australia

ACCOMPANIES: turkey, chicken, duck, shrimp, shellfish, cheese, green salad

The word "sauvignon" comes from the French "sauvage," meaning wild, a fitting descriptor for the flavor of the wine from this grape. To counter the intensity of the Sauvignon Blanc, it is often blended with the milder Sémillon grape.

SÉMILLON

TYPICAL STYLE: both dry and sweet
AROMAS: ripe fruit, nut, honey, orange peel
MOUTHFEEL: smooth
ACIDITY: medium
REGIONS: France (Bordeaux), Washington, Australia
ACCOMPANIES: white fish and fish stew, shellfish, foie gras, paté, cheese, dessert

The Sémillon grape is often blended with Sauvignon Blanc—its opposite—but can be used on its own. It is a component of some of the finest dessert wines, such as Sauternes.

OTHER IMPORTANT WHITES

GEWÜRZTRAMINER

TYPICAL STYLE: dry to mildly sweet

AROMAS: tropical fruits, spice

MOUTHFEEL: very smooth

ACIDITY: low to medium

REGIONS: France (Alsace), Germany, Washington, California, New York

ACCOMPANIES: turkey, veal, pork and pork products, fully-ripened cheeses

Gewürztraminer is perfect as a before-dinner drink, sensitizing the palate and encouraging the appetite, and a fine accompaniment to most Asian food. Late harvest Gewürztraminer expresses the deep, sweet aroma of the grape and is an exceptional treat with foie gras.

Moscato (Muscat)

Typical style: sweet, slightly sparkling
Aromas: grape, pear
Mouthfeel: smooth, sunny, full of grace
Acidity: high
Regions: Northern Italy, Spain, France, California
Accompanies: fruit, fruit tarts

Muscat is one of the rare varieties that produces a wine that actually smells like grapes. The best known wine made with Muscat grapes is Asti Spumante. It also is used as a table grape.

Pinot Blanc

Typical style: dry white
Aromas: slight apple, pear
Mouthfeel: smooth
Acidity: medium
Regions: France (Alsace), Italy (Tre Venezie), Germany, British Columbia,

California, Oregon
ACCOMPANIES: seafood, poultry, quiche

Pinot Blanc makes some very good wines that are soft and easy on the palate.

PINOT GRIS (GRIGIO)

TYPICAL STYLE: dry white
AROMAS: ripe fruit, apple, pear, melon, nut
MOUTHFEEL: soft, smooth
ACIDITY: medium
REGIONS: France (Alsace), Italy (Tre Venezie), Germany, Oregon, British Columbia
ACCOMPANIES: mildly spiced foods, salads, sandwiches

Both Pinot Blanc and Pinot Gris are lighter mutations of Pinot Noir. Pinot Gris can vary widely in taste, depending on where it is grown. In Italy, where it is called Pinot Grigio, it is a very simple, light, crisp wine, while, in Alsace, it is fuller and more dramatic. In Germany, where it is called Grauburgunder, it has a broader quality.

VIOGNIER

TYPICAL STYLE: dry white
AROMAS: apricot, exotic fruits, floral, spice
MOUTHFEEL: smooth
ACIDITY: low
REGIONS: France (Rhône Valley), Oregon, California
ACCOMPANIES: fruit and nut tarts, cheese

In the Rhône, Viognier grapes yield the prestigious Château-Grillet and Condrieu appellations. They are among the rarest, most superior French white grapes. A glass of Viognier is excellent before dinner.

MAin Red Varieties

CABERNET SAUVIGNON

TYPICAL STYLE: dry red
AROMAS: dark berries, blackberry, currant, cassis, cedarwood
MOUTHFEEL: smooth, with a coarse finish
ACIDITY: high
REGIONS: France (Bordeaux: Médoc), Italy, California, Australia
ACCOMPANIES: roast beef, venison, lamb, highly-fragrant cheeses

Cabernet Sauvignon makes a powerful wine that becomes silky and elegant with time. It has been described as sharp and "introverted" when young to full and highly flavorful in old age. This grape is the skeleton of the great wines of Bordeaux (Mouton and Lafite Rothschild), providing the structure of the wine in the mouth.

MERLOT

TYPICAL STYLE: dry red

AROMAS: plum, cherry, blackberry

MOUTHFEEL: soft

ACIDITY: medium

REGIONS: France (Bordeaux: St. Emilion, Pomerol), Italy, California, Washington State, Chile (often mixed with another variety called Carmenère)

ACCOMPANIES: game, beef, cheese

Merlot is often described as soft and plump, some of the characteristics that led it to be popular in the United States. It is a descendant of the Cabernet Franc grape, making it a close relation of Cabernet Sauvignon, with which it is often confused. Most Bordeaux are made of a blend of Cabernet Sauvignon and Merlot, with the latter providing the roundness of the wine. Château Petrus, one of the most expensive wines in the world, is 99% Merlot.

PINOT NOIR

TYPICAL STYLE: dry red

AROMAS: baked cherry, plum, damp earth

MOUTHFEEL: smooth, crisp finish

ACIDITY: high

REGIONS: France (Burgundy and Champagne), Oregon, California, New Zealand, Australia

ACCOMPANIES: lamb, pork, grilled salmon, game, beef stews, coq au vin; also on its own (as Champagne)

Pinot Noir can be grown and made into wine only in cool climate regions. For this reason, the grape is grown in smaller quantities than other varieties and is often expensive. In Burgundy, almost all red wine is made from the Pinot Noir, with the exception of Beaujolais. When grown in the right climate and the right soil, in Burgundy and Oregon, for example, it yields many of the finest, most aristocratic wines. Pinot

Noir is consistently referred to as sensual, even erotic, because of its silk-like mouthfeel and wonderfully earthy flavor. It is a major component of most Champagnes.

SYRAH (SHIRAZ)

TYPICAL STYLE: dry red
AROMAS: black pepper, blackberry
MOUTHFEEL: smooth, round
ACIDITY: medium to high
REGIONS: France (Rhône Valley), Australia, South Africa, Washington State, California
ACCOMPANIES: dark-meat poultry, red meats, venison, highly fragrant cheeses

Syrah is known as Shiraz in Australia and South Africa. It can be described as a virile, rustic, yet refined wine.

OTHER IMPORTANT REDS

BARBERA

TYPICAL STYLE: dry red
AROMAS: blackberry, black cherry, black raspberry, black plum
MOUTHFEEL: rather smooth
ACIDITY: high
REGIONS: Italy (Piedmont), Argentina, California
ACCOMPANIES: poultry, pizza

A flavorful, rich wine popular for everyday consumption.

CABERNET FRANC

TYPICAL STYLE: dry red
AROMAS: raspberry, strawberry, plum
MOUTHFEEL: rather smooth

ACIDITY: high
REGIONS: France (Loire Valley, Bordeaux),
Washington State, New York, California,
Argentina
ACCOMPANIES: lamb, beef, veal, flavorful
poultry, foie gras, cheese

GAMAY

TYPICAL STYLE: dry red
AROMAS: cherry
MOUTHFEEL: smooth
ACIDITY: high
REGIONS: France (Beaujolais)
ACCOMPANIES: charcuterie (preserved
meats), light lunches, milder cheeses

Gamay is used to make the French wine
Beaujolais.

GRENACHE

TYPICAL STYLE: dry red
AROMAS: ripe plum, cinnamon
MOUTHFEEL: smooth
ACIDITY: low to medium
REGIONS: California, Spain (Rioja), France (Rhône)
ACCOMPANIES: red meat, duck and other poultry

In France, Grenache is one of the grapes used in the excellent Châteauneuf-du-Pape wine.

SANGIOVESE

TYPICAL STYLE: dry red
AROMAS: cherry, orange peel
MOUTHFEEL: smooth
ACIDITY: high
REGIONS: Italy, California
ACCOMPANIES: salami, ham, veal, stronger-tasting poultry

The Sangiovese is Italy's most famous grape. Its best cultivations produce the great Chianti and Brunello di Montalcino wines.

TEMPRANILLO

TYPICAL STYLE: dry red
AROMAS: cherry, vanilla
MOUTHFEEL: smooth
ACIDITY: medium to high
REGIONS: Spain, Oregon
ACCOMPANIES: game, red meats, duck, bean ragouts

ZINFANDEL

TYPICAL STYLE: dry red
AROMAS: blackberry, boysenberry, plum
MOUTHFEEL: smooth
ACIDITY: medium
REGIONS: California
ACCOMPANIES: meat, duck, strongly-flavored cheeses

Although Zinfandel is grown almost exclusively in California, it has its origins in Europe (Croatia). This grape derives from the same species as Cabernet Sauvignon, Merlot, and Pinot Noir. It makes a wide variety of wines, from white to sweet Port-style.

decoding wine labels

DECODING WINE LABELS

There are four types of wine labels, each featuring a different sort of information——the variety of grape, country of origin, the region, and the producer—and many variations on these basic categories. In the U.S., health warnings are required by law.

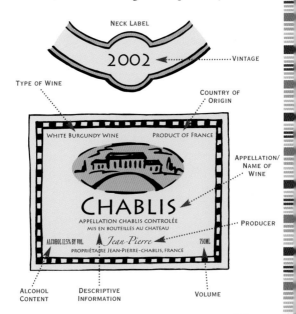

NECK LABEL

2002 ←........... VINTAGE

TYPE OF WINE

COUNTRY OF ORIGIN

WHITE BURGUNDY WINE   PRODUCT OF FRANCE

APPELLATION/ NAME OF WINE

CHABLIS
APPELLATION CHABLIS CONTROLÉE
MIS EN BOUTEILLES AU CHATEAU

ALCOHOL 12.5% BY VOL.   *Jean-Pierre*   750ML
PROPRIÉTAIRE JEAN-PIERRE-CHABLIS, FRANCE

PRODUCER

ALCOHOL CONTENT

DESCRIPTIVE INFORMATION

VOLUME

VARIETAL LABELS

These labels, which originated in California in the 1930s, feature most prominently the type of grape contained in the wine, such as Merlot or Zinfandel. The U.S., New Zealand, Australia, South Africa, and Argentina use this system. European producers use this type of labeling to compete in the U.S. market. California law requires that at least 75% of the wine must derive

from the grape featured on the label (and better quality wines contain closer to 100%); in Oregon the rule is 100%.

REGIONAL LABELS

European producers traditionally feature the place name on their labels, to indicate that the wine comes from a specific geographic area defined by law. A definite character is associated with the wine produced in each of these areas.

The principal European winemaking regions are made up of districts, which contain villages, which are in turn composed of specific vineyards. Certain celebrated American and Australian wines have begun to feature the regional name more prominently. The Appellation d'Origine Contrôlée classification system in France and other European wine categories are noted on this type of label.

PROPRIETARY LABELS

Winemakers have the right to use their names prominently on the label to create brand recognition for their customers. One prestigious example is Château Latour from Médoc in Bordeaux.

GENERIC LABELS

American and Australian winemakers have developed the practice of using the names of certain French regional wines for wines that they produce in the style of that particular region. They use the name Burgundy for a red of medium body, Chablis for a medium-dry white, and Champagne for a sparkling wine. These wines have little or nothing in common with the wines produced in the original region.

wines around the world

FRANCE

The French, second in volume of wine produced worldwide, have always considered place, or terroir—rather than the type of grape—to be the most important factor in the identity of a wine. Terroir is an amalgam of the soil composition and microclimate, as they derive from the local topography.

The government system for naming wines starts, at the top, with Appellation d'Origine Contrôlée. Appellation means naming, origine refers to where the wine originates, and contrôlée means "limited, prescribed, monitored." Many of  the best French wines carry this label; however, as with other wine laws around the world, the label AOC does not guarantee quality. It means rather that the grapes in the wine come from a specific area, and that only certain prescribed grapes have been used.

AOC also controls the minimum alcohol content of the wine, the maximum number of liters that can be produced per annum, how the vines are planted and pruned, and the methods used in fermenting and maturing (cask size, aging time, etc.). The wine may contain from one to over a dozen types of grapes, depending on the appellation. A wine that meets all the legal standards for a Bordeaux wine, for example, will bear the mention Appellation Bordeaux Contrôlée.

Beneath the AOC category in the French classification system comes Vin Délimité de Qualité Supérieure (VDQS) and then Vin de Pays, which includes many good wines, often exported to other countries. Vin de Table is the lowest category, covering nearly 40% of French wines, and means simply that the wine is red or white and the grapes were grown in France. The percentage of Vin de Table has decreased considerably over the last 50 years, due to an increase in demand for more sophisticated wines.

BORDEAUX

With a production of 700 million bottles of wine per year, Bordeaux is the biggest wine region in France. Geographically, the region is dominated by the large Gironde Estuary, fed by two important tributaries: the Dordogne and the Garonne.

More than any other region in France, Bordeaux is characterized by a wide range of wine styles, due to the higher number of grape varieties permitted. The most important red grapes are Merlot and Cabernet Sauvignon, but they are often blended with Cabernet Franc, Petit Verdot, and Malbec. Red Bordeaux dominate production, but grapes for white wine are also varied: Sémillon, Sauvignon Blanc, Muscadelle, Ugni Blanc. The ability to blend different types of grapes is what

gives the region's wines their deep, intense, and complex flavors, and trademark elegance. It is important to remember, however, that most Bordeaux are table wines of good quality, and only a small percentage rank among the finest wines in the world.

The famous Classification of 1855 originated in the Médoc—though it includes a few top wines from other regions—when Napoleon III ordered all Bordeaux wines to be classified for the Exposition Universelle in Paris. This system divided what were the best wines at the time into five crus, or growths, the Premier Cru, or first growth, indicating the highest quality wine. The classification has remained extremely rigid to this day: wines cannot change rank even if their quality improves or declines; thus some châteaux classified as fifth growths actually make first and second growth quality wines. The term Cru Bourgeois applies to all the châteaux that were not classified, and are generally simpler and less expensive than classified wines, though by no means poor. The unofficial term "super seconds" has emerged to designate excellent lower cru wines that can be compared to first and second growths. Note: many regions of Bordeaux not properly represented in 1855 have had to create their own classifications—as in Graves, St. Emilion, Sauternes and Barsac—and some regions aren't classified at all, such as Pomerol.

*Although the word "château" brings
to mind images of grandeur, in Bordeaux
it is used to designate any edifice,
from a small farmhouse to a castle,
and its surrounding vineyards.*

MÉDOC

Dominating the left bank of the Gironde, the Médoc is the largest wine-producing region in Bordeaux, most famous for its rich red wines. It is divided into two subregions—Médoc and Haut-Médoc. The latter, covering the southern part, is the more important wine region, and includes such famous appellations as St. Estèphe, Pauillac, Saint Julien, and Margaux. Many of the top red wines of the world come from this small area. Cabernet Sauvignon is the prominent grape, but it is always blended with Merlot and other Bordeaux

 grapes. The wines tend to have more body near the city of Bordeaux, becoming more "aristocratic" closer to the ocean.

St. Estèphe lies north of the gravelly southern Médoc villages, or communes, and its soil tends to have more clay, giving its wines a rugged character. The defining features of St. Estèphe derive from the high percentage of Merlot in the blend (*cépage*), which softens the effects of the soil. This commune's most sought-after wine is the rich Cos d'Estournel—a good example of a "super second"; others include Château Montrose and Calon-Ségur.

Pauillac has acquired a prestigious reputation as the birthplace of many of the finest classified wines, including three of the five first growths: Château Lafite-Rothschild, Château Latour, and Château Mouton-Rothschild. These wines, whether ample and full-bodied, or subtle and elegant, elicit elaborate descriptions and frank praise from those lucky enough to drink them. Châteaux Pichon Longueville Comtesse de Lalande, Lynch-Bages, d'Armailhac, and Haut-Batailley are among other top producers.

Saint Julien is the smallest Médoc appellation. Its wines are sought for their elegance and rich flavor. Some of the best estates include Château Léoville-Barton, Château Beychevelle, and Château Ducru-Beaucaillou. The wines of Margaux, the largest commune of the Médoc, are the most delicate and refined. Because of its southern location, Margaux is well-endowed in light, gravelly soil. Château Margaux is the leading estate, with others including Château Palmer, Rausan-Ségla, and Angludet.

GRAVES

The name "Graves" comes from the characteristic gravelly soil of the area, a feature that is advantageous in growing wine grapes as it allows easy drainage. The dominant red grape is the Cabernet Sauvignon, followed by Merlot and Cabernet Franc. Practically all of the white wines are made from a blend of Sémillon and Sauvignon Blanc. Graves is rather unique in that many of its châteaux produce both very fine white wines and, more recently, red wines. Reds bearing the Appellation Graves Contrôlée are often described as earthy, such as the Château Haut-Brion, the only Graves wine to be included in the Premier Cru of the 1855 Classification. With this exception, Graves has its own classification system of roughly thirteen red and ten white Cru Classé wines.

PESSAC-LÉOGNAN

Formerly part of Graves, the
northern Pessac-Léognan region
was formed into a new sub-
appellation in 1987. Many of
the best Graves wines now
appear under the Pessac-
Léognan appellation, including the reputed
Château Haut-Brion. Other great red and
white producing châteaux of the Graves and
Pessac-Léognan regions are Château La
Mission Haut-Brion, Château Bouscaut,
and Château Carbonnieux.

SAUTERNES AND BARSAC

South of Graves on the Garonne River are a
group of communes that produce sweet
wines almost exclusively. The most famous of
these are Sauternes and Barsac, which create
some of the finest dessert wines in the world.

The Sauternes and Barsac wines are mostly made from the Sémillon grape. The effects

 of the *botrytis* fungal disease as well as varied degrees of aging (5 to 30 years), greatly affect the taste, giving rise to delicious and complex apricot and honey flavored wines. Other great wines in the region include Châteaux Suduiraut, Rieussec, and Coutet, as well as the Lafaurie-Peyraguey and Guiraud estates.

ST. EMILION

A different, clay-based soil separates St. Emilion and Pomerol from the rest of wine-making Bordeaux and allows Merlot grapes, as well as Cabernet Franc, to flourish. Plum flavors pervade the finest wines. Omitted in the Classification of 1855, St. Emilion created its own system in 1954. The top wines are designated as Premier Grand Cru Classé, followed by Grand Cru Classé, and Grand Cru. This flexible system rates wines by quality every decade. The two most prestigious châteaux are Cheval Blanc and

Ausone. Other remarkable wines include Château Canon, Château Pavie, Château Magdelaine, and Château Angélus.

POMEROL

The Pomerol châteaux have only recently become famous, especially Petrus. For this reason, Pomerol has remained a small area with modest estates. Wines can be extremely expensive, as the small domains produce only a few hundred cases a year.

BURGUNDY

Wines in Burgundy are all about the individuality of the land, or terroir, they are grown on. This affects many aspects of the wine, including policies for blending and distribution of land among winemakers. Production is focused on two grapes: Pinot Noir for reds and Chardonnay for whites. Two exceptions are the white Aligoté occasionally used in blends—the sparkling Crémant de Bourgogne, for example —and the red Gamay used in Beaujolais.

Burgundy can be confusing, because it is significantly different from Bordeaux and has an extraordinary abundance of small wine-producing villages and winemaking estates. These factors date back to the medieval Benedictine monks who first separated the land into terroirs for wine cultivation.

As the basic unit for wine production in Bordeaux is the château, in Burgundy it is the domaine, often much smaller and more modest. In an effort to preserve the terroir of each wine, a vineyard is often divided among several owners, each owning a small parcel of land. A large domaine is not a single estate and its surrounding vineyards as in Bordeaux, but rather a collection of different parts of vineyards from various villages. In addition, not all wines are bottled by the vineyards. Merchants called négociants can purchase grapes from different vineyards, blend the wines from them, and sell them under their own name.

DID YOU KNOW?

In Burgundy, a single vineyard can have up to 90 owners, with some families owning holdings of only three or four rows of vines.

It is widely believed that the best, most elegant, and refined wines come from cooler climates, and this is one of the reasons why Burgundy wines are so great. The region possesses the ideal climate for Pinot Noir, a fragile and difficult grape to grow. However, the cool climate makes the grape especially prone to rot because of rain, or under-ripening if a planter has harvested early to avoid the rain. This is the reason, along with the small size of the domaines, why Burgundy's production is small—less than a quarter of that of Bordeaux—and why some top Burgundy wines are among the most expensive in the world.

Burgundy's classification system is as follows: the least prestigious wines are sold under the generic Appellation Contrôlée Bourgogne Blanc and Bourgogne Rouge. Next are the village wines, a step up in quality. Premier Cru wines are from better vineyards, and Grand Cru represents the crème de la crème.

Burgundy consists of five subregions: Chablis, Côte d'Or (including Côte de Beaune and Côte de Nuits), Côte Chalonnaise, the Mâconnais, and Beaujolais.

The cold, stark climate of CHABLIS, in the isolated most northern part of Burgundy, produces a crisp, delicate Chardonnay, which yields steely, dry white wines with a unique style. The wine produced in Chablis is most often fermented and aged in stainless steel tanks, preserving the wine's mineral gunflint character. Some producers use oak barrels for maturation in order to add an extra dimension of complexity to their wines. The best domains are situated on soil laced with limestone, such as the seven Grand Cru vineyards: Blanchot, Bougros, Grenouilles, Les Clos, Les Preuses, Valmur, and Vaudesir.

In the CÔTE D'OR, there are no less than thirty Grand Cru vineyards scattered among the villages of Côte de Nuits and Côte de Beaune, the Côte d'Or's north- ern and southern subregions. The "côte," or slope, is key here: a vineyard's status is determined by how high it sits on the hill. At the top, the Grand Cru and Premier Cru vineyards enjoy the best drainage, the most sun, and fine limestone soil.

The CÔTE DE NUITS produces mostly red wine. Its nine appellations are Chambolle-Musigny, Fixin, Flagey-Echézeaux, Gevrey-Chambertin, Marsannay, Morey-Saint Denis, Nuits-Saint-Georges, Vosne Romanée, and Vougeot. The CÔTE DE BEAUNE specializes in whites, but produces reds as well. Its appellations include Aloxe-Corton, Beaune, Chassagne-Montrachet, Meursault, Pommard, Puligny-Montrachet, Santenay, and Volnay.

> *The most famous estate of all
> is the Domaine de la Romanée-Conti,
> where certain vintages cost upwards
> of $1,000 a bottle.*

The main wine-producing villages of the CÔTE CHALONNAISE produce many slightly earthy Premier Cru wines. This is the place to go for good wines at a more affordable price. Mercurey is the best-known village, and the most expensive. It mostly produces a light and fruity red wine, and a few good whites. Mercurey's best wines are from Faiveley and Antonin Rodet. The village of Givry is known for sweet, pleasant, cherry-flavored reds such as those of Domaine Joblot, while the southern village of Montagny primarily makes Chardonnay. Bouzeron, in the north, is unique for its white Aligoté wines, especially those of Aubert de Villaine.

Last but not least is Rully, which makes good whites, notably the sparkling Crémant de Bourgogne. Its best producers include: Aubert de Villaine, Antonin Rodet, Domaine de la Folie, Domaine Joblot, Domaine de Suremain, Domaine Thénard, Domaine Veuve Steinmaier, Faiveley, and Louis Latour.

For good value in white Chardonnays, THE MÂCONNAIS, south of the Côte Chalonnaise, is ideal. Its best are Mâcon, Mâcon-Villages (better known villages attach their own name to the label, such as Mâcon-Lugny), Pouilly-Fuissé, and St.-Véran. These can be delicious at a reasonable price in good vintages, but overall they remain quite simple. Among the best Mâconnais producers are André Besson, Domaine Chenevière, Domaine Manciat-Poncet, Georges Duboeuf, Louis Jadot, Louis Latour, and Roger Lasserat.

BEAUJOLAIS, from the southernmost region of Burgundy, is the most un-Burgundy of Burgundies. The place and the wine both differ from the rest of the region. The climate is warmer, the grape is Gamay, and the soil is granite, rather than limestone. Most Beaujolais is light and playful, not as serious as its northern cousins. Despite its color, Beaujolais is in some ways more like a white wine than a red.

The best and richest Beaujolais are from designated villages, or crus, including Juliénas, Chénas, Moulin-à-Vent, Fleurie, Chiroubles, and Brouilly. Below these in quality are the Beaujolais-Villages, followed by the simple Beaujolais. These latter Beaujolais are simple, easy-drinking wines, but all Beaujolais remain light-hearted. Among the best producers are Brunet, Georges Duboeuf, Kermit Lynch, and Janin.

Beaujolais Nouveau is the fun party wine! Not only because of its young, vibrant grape flavors, but because it is meant to be drunk in celebration—specifically, celebration of the end of the harvest. By French law, this wine must be released on the third Thursday in November—just in time for Thanksgiving—and drunk no earlier than 12:01 A.M. on that date. Beaujolais Nouveau is meant to be enjoyed very young, within a year of its vintage.

Rhône Valley

The wines of the Rhône Valley are coarser and more rustic than the refined Bordeaux and Burgundies. The region is divided into north and south, each area producing its own style of wine. Northern wines, such as those from the appellations Côte-Rôtie ("roasted hillside") and Hermitage, are more sophisticated, but those of the south hold their own, boasting such beloved names as Châteauneuf du Pape. In the north, the principal red grape is Syrah, and the few whites that are produced come from Viognier, Roussane, and Marsanne. In the south, there are many more grape varieties. The south produces much white and rosé, as well as red; most Rhône wines come from the south. The generic appellation control is Côtes-du-Rhône (also Côtes-du-Rhône-Villages).

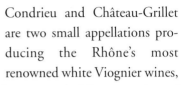

THE NORTHERN RHÔNE

Condrieu and Château-Grillet are two small appellations producing the Rhône's most renowned white Viognier wines, incredibly fragrant and delicate, tasting of peaches, apricots, melons, or honey. The Viognier vine is difficult to grow; thus yields are low, making the wines rare and expensive. Georges Vernay is the best-known producer of Condrieu. The tiny village of Château-Grillet is appellation and producer all in one. The St. Joseph appellation yields some great wines, softer than other Syrahs.

With the Côte-Rôtie, Hermitage is the top wine in the north, if not the whole Rhône. In the 18th and 19th centuries, it was more popular than the best Bordeaux and Burgundies. In recent years it has regained popularity as the boldest, most full-bodied, and masculine Syrah wine, a spicy, smoky red. The best producers are

Jean-Louis Chave, M. Chapoutier, Paul Jaboulet Aîné, and E. Guigal.

The Crozes-Hermitage, on the plains reaching out south and east of the Hermitage hill, is the largest appellation in the northern Rhône. These wines are similar to Hermitage and made from the same grapes, but tend to be lighter and less bold. Excellent producers are Alain Graillot, M. Chapoutier, and Paul Jaboulet Aîné. Cornas also produces powerful red wines from the Syrah grape in the rough and untamed style of Hermitage, but a little coarser.

THE SOUTHERN RHÔNE

Châteauneuf-du-Pape features fully fourteen wine grape varieties. The principal red is Grenache, followed by Syrah and Mourvèdre. This appellation is large, producing more than the entire northern Rhône. Châteauneuf-du-Pape inherited its name from Pope Clement V (14th c.), who established a papacy rivaling that of Rome in nearby Avignon. France's appellation system originated here as part of an effort to preserve the quality of regional wines. These reds are earthy and spicy, retaining the character of the terroir. There are many remarkable producers, including Château Rayas, Château de Beaucastel, Château La Nerthe, and Domaine du Vieux Télégraphe.

Gigondas wines, strong and vigorous, were awarded their appellation in 1971. They share blend and taste styles (raspberry) with

Châteauneuf-du-Pape, but are less refined. Château de Saint-Cosme, Domaine Les Pallières, and Domaine du Cayron are among the best. The wines of Vacqueyras are similar to Gigondas, but coarser and more rustic. Tavel produces rosé wines full of cherry and berry flavors. Despite their soft pink color, they are robust and rather coarse.

When uncorking a Champagne bottle, proper French etiquette dictates that the bang should be avoided. Instead, the bottle should make no more than a sigh.

CHAMPAGNE

No wine is more in demand for special occasions than the world-famous sparkling wine of Champagne. The vineyards of several subregions grow the three main grapes used in making this incomparable and festive beverage: Chardonnay brings elegance and refinement (Côte des Blancs); Pinot Noir, a red grape, provides structure and body (Montagne de Reims); and Pinot Meunier, also red, adds fruitiness and aroma (Montagne de Reims and Vallée de la Marne).

According to legend, Dom Pérignon, the Benedictine monk and cellar-master of the Abbey of Hautvillers, is the father of Champagne. In reality, he did not invent "bubbly," but made great strides in wine-making technique. He discovered that fermentation stopped during the winter, and that warmer spring weather triggered a second, bubble-generating fermentation. The admirable Dom was frustrated that he could not find a way to get rid of this pesky effervescence!

Several factors contribute to making this unique wine, as authentic Champagne can come only from this region. The vineyards, planted in chalky soil highly favorable to viticulture, are the most northern and coolest in France, yielding grapes high in acidity. The cool weather allows maturity without full ripening. Some growers produce their own

Champagne; most, however, do not, but own vineyards, and grow and harvest grapes. It is the "houses" that buy most of the grapes from the growers and make them into sparkling wines.

The quality of the grapes varies from year to year, depending on heat and sun. Non-vintage Champagnes, the bulk of production, provide the income. What counts in Champagne is not the quality of each individual wine, but the superiority of the final blend. Non-vintage Champagnes are a blend of 30 to 60 wines from different years that the blender estimates will complement each other after the bubble-generating second fermentation and finishing touches. Varying the origin of the grapes assures evenness in quality, and varying the years adds fullness. When making non-vintage Champagne, a master blender does not try to create the best possible blend, but one that is consistent and represents the style of the house.

In exceptionally good, sunny years, when the grapes ripen well, a house may choose to make a vintage Champagne from the best grapes of that year's harvest. These Champagnes must be aged longer to acquire the fullness that reserve wines add to non-vintage. Not every house declares a vintage the same year. Generally, only a few years of every decade are declared vintage years. Prestige Cuvées are exclusive and expensive. Only the very best grapes from the finest vineyards go into the blend.

Many different types of Champagne are produced. Each house has its own style, and different types of champagne within it. Blanc de Blancs literally means "white from whites" and designates Cham-pagne made exclusive-ly from Chardonnay. These wines tend to be light and fine and

more expensive because Chardonnay grapes are the most expensive in Champagne. Blancs de Noirs, exceptionally rare, are made entirely from one or both of the red grapes of Champagne. Champagnes vary in body—light and elegant to full—and sweetness. The dry Brut style is the most popular.

DOUX: intensely sweet, but virtually non-existent

DEMI-SEC: moderately sweet

SEC: slightly sweet

EXTRA DRY: off-dry/medium-dry

BRUT: varies between dry and very dry

EXTRA BRUT: completely dry

Among the best houses: Bollinger, Krug, Laurent-Perrier, Louis Roederer, Möet & Chandon, Perrier-Jouët, Pommery, Taittinger, and Veuve Clicquot.

LOIRE VALLEY

The Loire Valley stretches out along the Loire River from Sancerre in the east to the city of Nantes on the Atlantic. This, the longest river in France, was historically important for transporting goods such as wine across the country. The climate is cool, and many growers encounter problems ripening their grapes. Red, white, and rosé wines are produced, as well as sparkling and sweet, but the white wines are the most famous. The principal white grapes are Sauvignon Blanc and Chenin Blanc, and the main red is Cabernet Franc. There are three main wine-producing areas.

THE EASTERN LOIRE

The leading appellations of Sancerre and Pouilly Fumé are located on opposite banks of the Loire River, and produce some of the finest dry white

wines in the world. The Sauvignon Blanc grape is king here; growers embrace its wildness, high acidity, and piercing flavor. Sancerre produces spicy, grassy, herbal wines that are very crisp and refined. Some top producers are Domaine Henri Bourgeois, Lucien Crochet, and Domaine Henri Pelle.

The white eastern-bank wines of Pouilly Fumé are very similar, though slightly fuller, with smoky, gunflint flavors: de Ladoucette, Didier Dagueneau, and Domaine Laporte, for example.

THE CENTRAL LOIRE

An amazing variety of wines is made in Anjou-Saumur. The generic appellations, Anjou-Blanc, Rosé d'Anjou, and Anjou Rouge, dominate production. In top quality wines, the best-known appellation is Savennières, which produces dry whites from Chenin Blanc grapes, with honey and citrus flavors, considered among the best in the world. The small estate of Clos de la Coulée de Serrant is the most prestigious example.

The best rosés come from the more specific appellations of Cabernet d'Anjou, a rather sweet wine, and Rosé de Loire, a dry wine. The red wines of the region (Anjou-Villages, Saumur-Champigny) tend to be light and fruity. When the wine growers are lucky, the proper climatic elements combine to bring about the noble rot that affects the great Sauternes of Bordeaux. Dessert wines can also be made, such as Quarts de Chaume, Coteaux du Layon, and Bonnezeaux. After Champagne, Saumur is the most important sparkling wine producer in France.

The most famous appellation of Touraine is Vouvray, which has mastered the art of making white wine from Chenin Blanc grapes like no other place in the world. The area is unique for its chalky tuffeau limestone soil that was quarried to make the impressive châteaux that dot the countryside. In the caves left over from tuffeau mining, Vouvrays can age and improve an unusually long time for whites: up to 100 years! Two of the best are from Didier Champalou and Gaston Huet-Pinguet.

Touraine also produces simple red table wines, as well as Chinon, Bourgueil, and St.-Nicolas-de-Bourgueil—exceptionally light and flavorful Cabernet Franc reds.

THE WESTERN LOIRE

The region around the city of Nantes produces a dry, neutral wine, Muscadet, from grapes of the same name. The best Muscadets come from the sub-appellation of Muscadet de Sèvre-et-Maine, and are great matches for Atlantic seafood.

Many Muscadet bottles carry the words "sur lie" on the label. This means that the wine was left to rest on its lees, or fermentation yeasts, before being bottled, which gives the wine additional flavor, freshness, and a slight tingle on the tongue.

ALSACE

Protected by the Vosges Mountains, the region of Alsace in northeastern France has a mild, dry climate perfect for grapes. The majority of wines are dry, full-bodied whites. Alsace's history has been marked by constant struggle between France and Germany, and both have influenced wine production. Many grapes, such as Riesling and Gewürztraminer, are also widely grown in Germany. By law, Alsatian

winemakers must bottle their wines in flutes: slim, long-necked, German-style bottles. The name of the grape is allowed to appear on the label along with the Appellation Alsace Contrôlée.

Riesling is the most important grape. Alsace Rieslings are practically the opposite of their graceful, refined, and slightly sweet German counterparts. They are full-bodied and dry, with steel and mineral tastes; fruity overtones develop with a few years of aging. The extremely intense sensations of Gewürztraminer lead people to love or hate it. This wine has unbelievably bold fruity and spicy flavors that make for a wonderful experience if they are good—and the best are found in Alsace—but can easily be disappointing and flat.

Pinot Blanc, important to Alsace, is a

simple, light, and likeable wine, perfect for those who are intimidated by the bolder wines above. Another, Pinot Gris, sometimes called Tokay in Alsace, is a popular, full-bodied, spicy wine. Two varieties of Muscat exist, both dry: the more popular Muscat d'Alsace, and the lighter Muscat Blanc à petits grains. Pinot Noir, the only red wine made in Alsace, has greatly improved in the past two decades. In addition, one sparkling wine is made in the traditional Champagne method, the Crémant d'Alsace, usually from Pinot Blanc grapes only.

ITALY

Wine is a part of life in Italy. This country, smaller than California, produces around 30% of the world's wine, making it the world's top wine producer. Most Italian production is from domestic grapes that don't exist in other countries, and this creates confusion among people who wish to learn more about these wines.

Italian wine is made to go with food. The domestic Italian market consumes huge quantities of wine, which is one reason Italian winemakers have not traditionally felt market pressure to focus on quality. Italian production can be divided into two groups: the inexpensive wines, sold in larger bottles for everyday consumption, and the good ones, which represent a full range in quality up through the truly superior.

The Italian system for categorizing wines is based on the French appellation system, and the European Union two-level system.

Table wine in Italian is called *Vino da Tavola*. There are two groups. The simplest wines mention only "Italy." The label for the Indicazione di Geografica Tipica (IGT) wines mentions a specific geographic location; these are of higher, sometimes very good, quality.

Within the higher-level EU category, known as Quality Wines Produced in a Specific Region (QWPSR), there are also two groups of wines: Denominazione di Origine Controllata (DOC), and the superior Denominazione di Origine Controllata e Garantita (DOCG), which must pass a taste test and be bottled in the same area in which the grapes are grown and fermented.

Italy has a vast range of soils and climates, and for that reason yields an immense variety of wines. There are 20 general wine regions in Italy, of which three are especially important. In Italy, as elsewhere, the best wines come from vineyards located on well-drained slopes of relatively infertile soil.

PIEDMONT

The term "piedmont" refers to the location of this region at the foot of the mountains—the Alps—in the northwest of Italy. Nearly 18% of the Italian QWPSR wines are produced here. Two of the best red wines worldwide come from the Nebbiolo grape, grown only in this area. Barolo and Barbaresco are both DOCG wines produced in the hilly Langhe area around Alba. These robust, highly structured, very dry reds are similar in many respects. Notes of strawberry and raspberry, rose, prune, violet, licorice, and tar predominate, and acid and tannin levels are high. They require significant aging. Barbaresco is generally lighter, less masculine, and is not aged quite as long. Buying these wines from a good producer is important. A handful from the many good ones includes Bruno Ceretto, Angelo Gaja, Bruno Giacosa, Giuseppe Mascarello, and Giuseppe Rinaldi.

The most important grape in the Piedmont is the traditional Moscato, used to produce the elegant Moscato d'Asti, and the well-known, sweetish and sparkling Asti, formerly known as Asti Spumante, not always consistent in quality. Barbera is another favorite, a flavorful red, much less tannic than Barolo and Barbaresco, and requiring far less aging. Because of its high acid content, this wine is vibrant and

alive, with aromas of chocolate and black cherry. The Barbera grape is the second most common grape in Italy after the Sangiovese, and yields especially delicious wines in Piedmont, particularly around Alba and Asti. Low in acid and lighter in body than Barbera, the Dolcetto wine, made from the grape of the same name, is pleasant and easy to drink. A few producers, such as Chionetti and Vietti, are dedicated to making top-notch Dolcetto.

TRE VENEZIE

The name Three Venices comes from the former Venetian Empire. This region in the northeastern part of Italy loosely groups three major wine-producing areas.

Between Venice and Lake Garda, and centered around Verona, lies THE VENETO, home to three well-known wines which in the past were not always of the best quality. The white Soave is produced from the Trebbiano grape. For good examples of this often dull, lackluster wine, it is best to seek out vineyards close to the town of Soave. The reds of the area, Valpolicella and Bardolino, have also been overproduced. The light, almost pink, easy-to-drink Bardolino has pleasant cherry and soft spice flavors especially appreciated in the summer. From the Amarone classico subdistrict comes a richer, full-bodied wine, high in alcohol, made by drying the super-ripe grapes over the winter until they are shriveled to concentrate their sugar and aromas. Amarone, which is not an inexpensive wine, emanates earthy, dried-fruit flavors, reminiscent of Port.

The second area in the Tre Venezie, situated between the Veneto and the Balkan frontier, is FRUILI-VENEZIA GIULIA, which has

become known in the past few decades for its white wines, though it also produces decent reds. The eastern-most hilly areas are responsible for the best of these. Friulian white wines are loaded with personality, and typically feature notes of fruit and spice. The bold, medium-bodied Tocai Friulano is particularly appreciated by the people of the region. One exceptional, though expensive, full-bodied white is Vintage Tunina, produced by Jermann; a few of the other quality producers in the area include EnoFriulia, Pierpaolo Pecorari, Ronco del Gnemiz, and Ronco dei Tassi.

In the northernmost part of Italy lies the mountainous TRENTINO-ALTO ADIGE, which combines two very different regions with correspondingly varied wines. This spectacularly beautiful region grows an unusually large variety of grapes, both domestic and international. The German-speaking Alto Adige exports very good white wines, rivaling those of neighboring Friuli. In Trentino, the Italian-speaking southern part of the region, the local Teroldego grape is used to produce Teroldego Rotaliano, a notable fruity red wine.

TUSCANY

This stunning and well-traveled region of undulating hills produces one of Italy's most famous red wines: the very dry, cherry and violet-scented Chianti. The DOCG wine zone covers much of the region, with, at its heart, the Chianti Classico, which—along with Chianti Rufina—produces the best wines. Chianti Riserva is aged in barrels of French oak for a minimum of three years, and can benefit from further aging in the bottle for a considerable number of years. Chianti today is higher in quality than ever before, and its price is still reasonable. Chianti wines by law must be made of at least 90% Sangiovese and Canaiolo grapes.

The same Sangiovese grape produces a relative newcomer, the Brunello di Montalcino, with its pronounced woodsy aroma and notes of licorice. This pricey DOCG wine holds its place among the best and longest-aging reds in the world. A new generation of winemakers has produced new red wines using Cabernet Sauvignon and Cabernet Franc grapes along with the traditional Sangiovese. These wines, known as Super Tuscans, can be very good and very expensive; fine examples are Sassicaia and Ornellaia.

SPAIN

Spain's wide variety of climate areas permits it to produce a broad variety of wine styles, from full-bodied reds and gentle whites to the fortified Sherries of the south. Like Australia, Spain is endowed with extremes of climate. The coast is generally cool in the north, and equatorially influenced towards the south. The center is completely dry and desert-like. A startling fact: Spain has more square miles of vineyard than any country in the world. Yet it is third in production after Italy and France, because of extremely high temperatures. After remaining on the sidelines for many decades, Spain has recently come of age in the modern wine world.

RIOJA is Spain's premier winemaking area, and, in Rioja, the early-ripening

Tempranillo grape (from *temprano,* early) is king. This area in the northeast of the country is divided into regions according to how much chalk there is in the soil, with the chalkiest vineyards yielding the best wines. About 75% of wines produced are red. These most often include a blend with one or more of the other permitted grapes: Graciano, Garnacha (Grenache), and Mazuelo. In earlier times Rioja reds were aged for years in American oak barrels, which tended to dull the wines and diminish their fruitiness. New bottle-aged Riojas are fresher and fruitier. Top producers include: La Rioja Alta, Bodegas Montecillo, and Marqués de Murrieta Ygay. In the shadow of its famous neighbor, NAVARRA, to the northeast, makes wines comparable to those of Rioja, but relatively less expensive.

The inaccessible region of PRIORATO, in Catalonia, has recently made winemaking news. Old vine stock of Garnacha and

Carignan is now producing full, robust red wines, high in tannin and alcohol, from the infertile volcanic soil in this region harshly continental in climate. Yields are tiny and these wines are expensive. They generally require aging to make them more approachable. Another Catalonian wine area is PENEDÈS, where the Torres family pioneered temperature-controlled fermentation in the '70s, and planted numerous classical French grape varieties, such as Cabernet Sauvignon and Merlot, as well as local Tempranillos and others. The red wines are often the best in quality. This region is also known for its Cava, a sparkling wine made from the Champagne method, which has recently begun to include Char-donnay in its blend, yielding a lively, inexpensive wine.

Several hours north of Madrid lies the RIBERA DEL

DUERO, where the Tempranillo grape yields perhaps its ultimate in Spanish wines. These dark, full-bodied wines, velvety when left to age, are produced notably by Vega Sicilia, whose Unico is the best-known high-end Spanish wine. To the west lies RUEDA, the country of Cervantes, and the burial place of Columbus. The producer Marqués de Riscal makes one of the best examples of the top-quality, fresh white wines made here from the Verdejo grape. In the northwest of Spain, in Galicia, RÍAS BAIXAS produces a wonderful new white wine, Albariño.

In JEREZ, on the coast of southern Spain, is produced the famous Sherry wine often served as an aperitif. The coastal location helped the export trade in this fortified wine that, in Tudor times, was already mentioned by Shakespeare as the wine of Falstaff.

PORTUGAL

Portugal has been famous traditionally for its excellent dessert wine, Port (Porto), which is fortified with brandy. The country now produces top-quality dry reds as well, mostly from local grape varieties. One of the best is from the same area where Port is produced: the full-bodied Barca Velha, from the DOURO region. Douro produces numerous smooth, ripe-flavored red wines of excellent value. In the northwest corner of Portugal, winemakers of THE MINHO produce the slightly effervescent, highly acidic Vinho Verde (green wine), a refreshing white perfect for drinking in hot climates. The region of DAO produces soft wines, including ripe, floral reds and nut-flavored whites.

GERMANY

There are many high quality, attractive wines in this country, which in recent times has been the victim of wine fashions and stereotypes. Despite popular beliefs, all German wines are not sweet whites, though whites, including dry whites, are the German specialty. As the climate is unpredictable, the vintage is particularly important in assessing German wines.

German winemakers do not use the French-based appellation system, but have their own system, in which the ripest grapes with the highest sugar content receive the

highest rating. Wines are named after the village and vineyard they come from, with the grape name usually included at the end. Labels with a lower alcohol content will usually indicate a sweeter wine. The word *trocken* on the label means "dry."

The Riesling grape thrives in the cooler German temperatures. Other grapes include Müller-Thurgau, Silvaner, Kerner, and Grauburgunder (Pinot Gris). Germany's sweet dessert wines are among the best in the world. They are produced both from *botrytis* (noble rot) and by the late harvesting of grapes (ice wines). Inexpensive German whites are appealingly light and fruity.

The enchantingly picturesque MOSEL-SAAR-RUWER region centers on the meandering Mosel River. Classic Rieslings are produced here, with their trademark high acidity plus a touch of sweetness. These Mosel wines in their distinctive green bottles strike a perfect balance between fruitiness and freshness. Top producers include Egon Müller, Karlsmühle, Alfred Merkelbach,

Willi Schaefer, and Zilliken. Nearby
RHEINGAU whites (over 80% Riesling) are
dry and earthy, with citrus aromas and none
of the sweetness of the Mosel wines. THE
RHEINHESSEN is the biggest wine-producing region in Germany. Many of the wines
produced here, including the well-known
Liebfraumilch, are simple, pleasing everyday
whites. The most widely-planted grape is
Müller-Thurgau. Sunny weather in THE
PFALZ region produces relatively rich, full-
bodied white wines, with ripe-fruit aromas, as
well as very good red wines.

Germany's other
notable wine regions
include: MITTELRHEIN,
AHR, NAHE, FRANKEN,
and BADEN.

AUSTRIA

In recent times, Austria has made its name as a high-quality wine producer. There is an Austrian grape, the Grüner Veltliner, which makes a full-bodied, crisp, slightly spicy white wine, but the nation is also well known for excellent Rieslings, both dry and sweet. Main regions include LOWER AUSTRIA, VIENNA, BURGENLAND, and STYRIA. Less than 30% of Austrian wines are red; these originate principally in Burgenland. The labels are similar to those of Germany.

U.S.A.

With virtually every type of climate, the United States is home to many different types of wine. The industry is diverse and growing fast, but this is a recent phenomenon.

Wine producing in the U.S. got off to a rough start. The first wine growers on the east coast encountered many difficulties: native grape varieties did not make good wine, and imported vines from Europe died quickly from phylloxera, the tiny, root-feeding aphid. The west coast fared better. Many people  consider the Hungarian grower Agoston Haraszthy to have started the boom by successfully planting many thousands of vine cuttings that he had sent to California from Europe in the 1860s. Events in the first half of the 20th century—two world wars, the Depression, and Prohibition—severely damaged the wine industry. Since the 1970s, however, wine has blossomed—the U.S. has become the fourth producer worldwide. California is responsible for roughly 90% of U.S. production.

American wine laws are much less restrictive than the French regulations, thus allowing winemakers to innovate. The backbone of these laws is the system of American Viticultural Areas (AVAs), which geographically delimits areas of production. The AVAs do not set restrictions on what grape varieties can be grown where, but a wine from a certain AVA must include no less than 85% of grapes from that particular area. If a variety is indicated on the bottle, the wine must contain at least 75% of that variety. If a vintage is featured, 95% of the wine must originate in that vintage year.

Klamath River
Goose Lake
Shasta Lake
Sacramento River
Mendocino
Lake County
Napa Valley
Sonoma County
Carneros
Sierra Foothills
Lake Tahoe
Nevada
Sacramento
Mono Lake
Oakland
San Francisco
Livermore Valley
San Jose
San Joaquin River
Northern Central Coast
Monterey
Carmel
Salinas
Fresno
Middle and Southern Central Coast
Pacific Ocean
Santa Maria Valley
Santa Ynez Valley
Santa Barbara
Los Angeles
San Diego

CALIFORNIA

The history of wine in California started with the early Spanish missionaries who brought "mission grapes" north from Mexico to make wines for settlers and sacramental ceremonies.

The state's varied climate, especially in the cooler areas, allows for diverse and interesting wines. The trademark fog of the San Francisco Bay area ameliorates the intense heat, and renders stretches of land further inland perfect for grape-growing. California's leading grapes are Chardonnay, Sauvignon Blanc, Cabernet Sauvignon, Merlot, Pinot Noir, and Zinfandel (and the wines are called by the name of the grape).

California dazzled the wine world when, at the Paris tasting of 1976, its wines won first place for both red and white, defeating the top French wines in a blind tasting.

The NAPA VALLEY is the most prestigious winemaking region in the U.S. It accounts for less than 5% of California's total production, but boasts a high proportion of fine wines. The best wine here is Cabernet Sauvignon, but Napa wineries also produce wine from the five other varieties, as well as blends from minor Bordeaux varieties (Cabernet Franc, Malbec, Petit Verdot), often called Meritage, which are among the most complex and interesting wines.

Within the Napa Valley AVA are 13 smaller AVAs that cover most of the valley as well as parts of the surrounding mountains. These are Rutherford, Oakville, Yountville, St. Helena, Wild Horse Valley, Chiles Valley, Howell Mountain, Stags Leap District, Atlas Peak, Spring Mountain, Diamond Mountain, Mount Veeder, and Carneros (part Napa, part Sonoma). The quality

of the soil and type of climate vary tremendously from one area to another, making Napa wines exceptionally diverse.

During the California Gold Rush in the mid 1800s, a Finnish sea captain named Gustave Niebaum founded one of the state's most famous wineries: Inglenook. Little did he know that just over 100 years later it would be sold to Francis Ford Coppola. The estate now goes by the name of Niebaum-Coppola and makes a fine Meritage wine called Rubicon.

Here are some of the best Napa Valley wineries: Beaulieu Vineyard (Cabernet Sauvignon), Beringer Vineyards, Cakebread Cellars, Caymus Vineyard, Clos du Val, Diamond Creek, Dominus Estate, Dunn Vineyards, Grgich Hills Cellar, Mason Vineyards, Mayacamas Vineyards, Robert

Mondavi, Opus One, Joseph Phelps Vineyards, Pride Mountain Vineyards, Shafer Vineyards, Silverado Vineyards, Stag's Leap Wine Cellars, Stags' Leap Winery, Stony Hill Vineyard, Trefethen Vineyards.

The climate and topography of **SONOMA COUNTY** are similar to those of the Napa Valley, but in character, the two viticultural areas couldn't be more different. While Napa is characterized by glamorous names and luxurious estates, the lesser-known Sonoma County remains rural and rustic, with an easygoing attitude. Many of Sonoma's wineries are family owned and run. Sonoma is larger than the Napa Valley, but does not have as many wine businesses, nor are they as concentrated. Many small farmers prosper here among the vineyards.

Sonoma County includes twelve smaller AVAs, some existing within each other. The most important are the Russian River Valley, Green Valley, Chalk Hill, Alexander Valley, Dry Creek Valley, Sonoma Valley, and Sonoma Mountain. These viticultural areas vary in climate, leading to a diversified production. While Cabernet Sauvignon prospers in the warm Alexander Valley, Pinot Noir and Chardonnay flourish in the cooler climate of the Russian River Valley.

Some of the best wineries in Sonoma County are Arrowood Vineyards, Davis Bynum Winery, Chalk Hill Estate Vineyards and Winery, Chateau St. Jean, Ferrari-Carano, Foppiano Vineyards, E. & J. Gallo, Hartford Court, Kistler Vineyards, Laurel Glenn Vineyards, Marcassin, Marimar Torres Estate, Matanzas Creek Winery, Peter Michael Winery, A. Rafanelli Winery, Ravenswood, J. Rochioli Vineyard, Joseph Swan Vineyards, and Williams & Selyem Winery.

CARNEROS is a small region straddling

southern Sonoma County and the Napa Valley. Because of its location, Carneros benefits from cool breezes sweeping up from the San Francisco Bay. These conditions are perfect for making elegant Chardonnays and Pinot Noirs. Sparkling wines are also made from these grapes, and famous French Champagne houses such as Taittinger and Chandon and Spanish Cava giant Freixenet own shares of local vineyards. Leading wineries include Domaine Carneros, Acacia Winery, Etude, and Saintsbury.

MENDOCINO COUNTY, LAKE COUNTY, and THE SIERRA FOOTHILLS are located to the north and northwest of Sonoma County and the Napa Valley. As in Carneros, Mendocino and Lake counties are rather cool areas favorable to growing such grape varieties as Chardonnay, Pinot Noir, Riesling, and Gewürztraminer. The famous French Roederer Champagne house and Pacific Echo owned by LVMH (Möet Hennessy Louis

Vuitton) produce sparkling wines in the cool Anderson Valley of Mendocino County. The Sierra Foothills are a warmer area, and winemakers compensate by placing their wineries at higher altitudes. At 3,000 feet, the Madrona Vineyards are believed to be the highest in the state. The leading grape in the Sierra Foothills is Zinfandel, a variety well suited for warm weather.

These three AVAs are perhaps the most rural wine producing areas in California. The Foothills are especially rugged. Surprisingly, two of the largest wineries in the state are based in Mendocino and Lake counties, using technologically advanced methods for winemaking.

Vineyards were first planted in the Sierra Foothills during the California Gold Rush in 1849, for the benefit of pioneering miners.

Some of the best wineries here are Roederer Estate, Guenoc Estate Vineyards, and Steele Wines in Mendocino County; Navarro Vineyards, McDowell Valley Vineyards, and Lolonis Winery in Lake County; and Montevina, Renwood Winery, and Sobon Estate in the Sierra Foothills.

In the Central Coast area, the Livermore and Santa Clara valleys benefited much from their proximity to San Francisco in the past and were once important, prosperous, wine producing regions; now they are slowly being overrun by suburbanization. Still, some of the remaining wineries in this area make fine wines from Sauvignon Blanc, Sémillon, and Chardonnay grapes. The LIVERMORE VALLEY's best wineries are Concannon Vineyard, Wente Vineyards, Cedar Mountain, and Murrieta's Well; Santa Clara Valley's best are J. Lohr Winery and Mirassou.

The ruggedly beautiful Santa Cruz Mountains, in the NORTHERN CENTRAL COAST region, produce four main grapes. On the cool ocean side Pinot Noir and Chardonnay dominate, while the warmer side facing the valley produces Zinfandel and Cabernet Sauvignon. Some of the top wineries of the Santa Cruz Mountains are Bonny Doon Vineyard, David Bruce Winery, Mount Eden Vineyards, Thomas Fogarty, and the Santa Cruz Mountain Vineyard.

Many winemakers have been attracted to the Northern Central Coast's picturesque Monterey County to escape the expansion of the suburbs in Livermore and Santa Clara. Monterey County is dominated by vast farming areas, but the number of wineries is growing. In the cooler northern parts, Rieslings and Chardonnays are made, while, as usual, Pinot Noir, Cabernet Sauvignon,

and Merlot dominate the warmer southern regions. If the vines are not properly tended, the wines can take on an undesirable herbal, vegetal taste, reminiscent of Monterey's agricultural side. Among the top wineries are Chalone Vineyard, Chateau Julien, Estancia Vineyards, Morgan Winery, and Paraiso Springs Vineyard.

In San Luis Obispo County of the MIDDLE AND SOUTHERN CENTRAL COAST are located the AVAs of Paso Robles, Edna Valley and Arroyo Grande. Paso Robles is located in the middle of the Central Coast and is its warmest area, so the leading grapes here are Cabernet Sauvignon and Zinfandel. Paso Robles wineries are also trying out some Rhône blends. In contrast, the Edna Valley and the Arroyo Grande benefit from the cool Pacific breezes and are best adapted to producing Chardonnay, Pinot Noir, as well as a bit of Viognier. Some of Paso Robles' best wineries are Peachy Canyon Winery, Eberle

Winery, Meridian Vineyards, and Wild Horse Vineyards. In the Edna Valley and the Arroyo Grande, look for Alban Vineyards (for Viognier), Edna Valley Vineyards, and Talley Vineyards.

Two valleys in Santa Barbara County—Santa Maria and Santa Ynez—are unique in that they run from east to west. These are perfect corridors for the cool winds from the ocean, and the average summer temperature is 75 degrees. Very fine, crisp Chardonnays and Pinot Noirs can be found here, as well as Riesling in the Santa Ynez Valley. Wineries to look for are Au Bon Climat, Byron Vineyards, Foxen Vineyard, Qupé Cellars, and Zaca Mesa Winery.

OREGON

The wine industry came to Oregon in the early 1960s, with the opening of Hillcrest Vineyard. At the same time, the first Pinot Noir vines were planted by Eyrie Vineyards—a landmark event for Oregon's wine world, as the Burgundian grape has found a second home here. Although it is still young, Oregon's wine industry is receiving worldwide recognition for its wines, especially Pinot Noir, well suited for Oregon's cooler climate.

The most important wine region is the WILLAMETTE VALLEY. It leads the state in production, mostly of Pinot Noir and Chardonnay. However, a new wine is creating much excitement: Pinot Gris. Two regions  of note to the south are the UMPQUA and ROGUE VALLEYS, slightly warmer, which grow Cabernet

Sauvignon, Syrah, and Merlot. In the north are Oregon's two smallest regions: COLUMBIA VALLEY and WALLA WALLA.

Some of Oregon's best wineries (and the number is growing rapidly) are Andrew Rich Wines, Adelsheim Vineyards, Archery Summit, Beaux Freres, Broadley Vineyards, Chehalem, Domaine Drouhin Oregon, Domaine Meriwether, Erath Vineyards, Eyrie Vineyards, Hamacher Wines, King Estate, Penner Ash Wines, Ponzi Vineyards, and Willakenzie Estates.

WASHINGTON

Washington is a relative newcomer to the wine world and has experienced incredible growth since the 1980s. Seattle's famous rainy weather would seem to negate the idea that wine could be grown here, but the state is actually the second producer in the country. The key to Washington's success is the Cascade Mountains: the western rains are blocked by the mountains, creating a dry, almost barren, continental climate on the eastern side. Most appellations are located in eastern Washington and all vineyards require irriga-

tion (except the less important PUGET SOUND region to the west). The largest AVA is the huge COLUMBIA VALLEY. Inside are the smaller AVAs of WALLA WALLA and YAKIMA VALLEYS; the latter has the most wineries and includes the RED MOUNTAIN AVA.

Washington's leading varietal wines are Merlot and Cabernet Sauvignon, followed by Sauvignon Blanc, Cabernet Franc, Riesling, Sémillon, Syrah, and Chardonnay. Washington also makes wine from the Lemberger grape from Germany. This curious exception to the usual vinifera varieties makes surprisingly good fruity red wines. The biggest winery in Washington is Chateau Ste. Michelle, but there are many excellent small businesses. Among Washington's best are Andrew Will Winery, Arbor Crest Wine Cellars, Château Ste. Michelle, Chinook Wines, DeLille Cellars, Hedges Cellars, The Hogue Cellars, Leonetti Cellar, Paul Thomas, Quilceda Creek Vintners, and Snoqualmie Vineyards.

NEW YORK

New York winemaking predates that of California, but has failed to develop in a major way. Disease ravaged the first plantings of the settlers, and the imposition of Prohibition was a blow just as the area was establishing itself. Other difficulties include cold weather and early frosts. To compensate, winemakers plant their vines close to large bodies of water—the Finger Lakes, the Hudson River—where the weather is more moderate.

New York State has a uniquely diverse set of grapes. Not only are the traditional European (*vitis vinifera*) varieties grown—Chardonnay, Riesling, Cabernet Sauvignon, and Merlot—but native varieties (*vitis labrusca*) and French-American hybrids as well. The native grapes include Concord—the most common, used mainly for juice and jam—Catawba, Niagara, and Delaware. Some of the hybrids include Seyval Blanc, Vidal Blanc, Cayuga, and Baco Noir. New York has three major wine producing regions: the Finger Lakes, the Hudson River Valley, and Long Island.

Responsible for approximately 80 percent of New York's production, **THE FINGER LAKES** is the major wine region. This area has inherited Iroquois names such as Canandaigua, the name of New York's largest wine producing company and one of the largest in the country. Most wineries in the state, however, are small family-run businesses. European and hybrid varieties dominate. Some of the finest wineries are Dr. Frank's Vinifera Wine Cellars, Fox Run Vineyards, Glenora Wine Cellars, Lamoreaux Landing Wine Cellars, Standing Stone Vineyards, and Swedish Hill Vineyard.

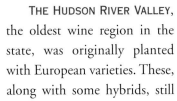

THE HUDSON RIVER VALLEY, the oldest wine region in the state, was originally planted with European varieties. These, along with some hybrids, still grow there today. Some vineyards to look for are Benmarl Vineyards, Brotherhood Winery, Magnanini Winery, and Millbrook Vineyards.

The wine history of LONG ISLAND began in 1973, when Louisa and Alex Hargrave discovered the North Fork's wine-growing potential. This very sunny region is perfect for warm weather grapes such as Merlot and Cabernet Sauvignon. Though the few wineries here are all recent, this is New York's most prestigious wine region because of the Hamptons, the popular weekend get-away of rich Manhattanites. Wineries include Bedell Cellars, Channing Daughters Winery, Lenz Winery, Palmer Vineyards, and Pellegrini Vineyards.

AUSTRALIA

Australia is the Brave New World of wine production, one of the most technologically advanced wine countries in the world and number seven in quantity produced. Very pleasant, fruity wines at reasonable prices make Australian wines broadly popular. The principal grape used in the top wines is Shiraz, the local name for Syrah; Chardonnay is the number one white grape for fine wines. Other grapes include Riesling, Sémillon, and Cabernet Sauvignon. Varietal labels are most often used, with 85% minimum content of the grape by law. The best areas for wine production are in the southern part of the country, where the climate is warm, but cooler than other areas, and dry.

Three principal wine producing

regions are known collectively as Southeastern Australia. The top producer in terms of volume is the state of SOUTH AUSTRALIA, with a wide variety of styles, from robust Shiraz to delicate Pinot Noir. The best of these wines are made close to the capital, Adelaide. For example, the warm Barossa Valley area, home of the huge Penfolds winery, and the district of McLaren Vale both produce the unusual blend Cabernet-Shiraz appreciated around the globe. Also here are Clare Valley, which produces the finest Rieslings in Australia, and Coonawarra, often considered the most unique terroir in Australia, with its bright red soil, well-drained limestone substratum, and constant, shallow water table. Coonawarra yields some of the country's best Cabernet Sauvignons, which rival the top Napa Valley Cabernets.

The second region is NEW SOUTH

WALES, which produces vast amounts of table wine, as well as excellent Sémillons in the subtropical Lower Hunter Valley, fat Chardonnays in Upper Hunter Valley, and reds in Mudgee.

The third region is VICTORIA, home to many smaller producers. Here, Rutherglen produces an Australian rendition of the fortified sweet Port wine known as Liqueur Muscat with its aromas of prune and fig. In the cooler southern areas of the state such as Yarra Valley, cool weather grapes (Riesling, Pinot Noir, Chardonnay) thrive, as well as Bordeaux Cabernets and Merlots. High-quality traditional sparkling wines are also made here. Goulburn Valley is famous for full-bodied Shiraz.

Australia's other two—and more remote—wine regions include TASMANIA, home to a burgeoning sparkling wine industry, and WESTERN AUSTRALIA, with its ever-growing viticultural diversity.

NEW ZEALAND

Winemaking is relatively new in the two main islands that form New Zealand, despite a highly suitable maritime climate, but production is increasing annually. This southernmost wine-producing country has ample sun and cool evening temperatures, which contribute to an especially fruity, crisp, lively wine style, particularly in Sauvignon Blanc. Intense, highly acid, and unique Sauvignon Blancs, with aromas of lime, passion fruit, and gooseberry, are responsible for the rise

to fame of MARLBOROUGH, on South Island, which also produces Chardonnays. Pinot Noir, the most common red grape in the country, is grown on both islands, with especially impressive results in the

North Island region of MARTINBOROUGH, where the wine takes on a refined, silky texture, and CENTRAL OTAGO, well south of Marlborough. Good Chardonnays are also grown in GISBORNE, in the northeastern tip of North Island. South of there, HAWKE'S BAY yields top-notch Cabernet Sauvignons.

In the north of North Island, the wine region of AUCKLAND and its environs is home to many wineries and wine company headquarters. On South Island, NELSON and CANTERBURY round off New Zealand's wine regions with characteristic beauty and favorable climate.

SOUTH AFRICA

South Africa is the oldest vine-growing country outside Europe. Most of the everyday wines come from the coastal region, near the Cape of Good Hope. The principal wine-producing districts of **FRANSCHHOEK VALLEY**, **PAARL**, **ROBERTSON**, **STELLENBOSCH**, and **CONSTANTIA** offer a wide variety of growing conditions and microclimates. Chenin Blanc, known as Steen in South Africa, has been the most widely planted grape. Increasingly popular is the uniquely South African Pinotage wine produced from its grape namesake—a genetic cross between Pinot Noir and Cinsault. Vineyard plantings have expanded recently with rapidly improving wine quality and export to world markets. Best producers include Charles Beck, de Tour, and Villiera.

ARGENTINA

Argentina grows wine principally in the area west of the Andes, and mostly in the state of Mendoza. **LA RIOJA**, the oldest wine region, produces Argentina's most famous white wine, the Torrontés. The dominant red wine grapes are the Bordeaux variety, Malbec (grown most notably in the country's leading wine region of **MENDOZA**), and Cabernet Sauvignon. Catenan Estate is one of the finest producers. **SAN JUAN**, located between La Rioja and Mendoza, is Argentina's second most prolific wine region. **SALTA**, to the north, specializes in Torrontés and Cabernet Sauvignon. Argentinian wines are an excellent value.

CHILE

Chile has been producing wine since the mid 16th century, but the industry has exploded since the 1980s. Many vineyards are situated in the Central Valley, with MAULE, RAPEL, and MAIPO the principal regions there. The focus in Chilean cultivation is on the French grapes Merlot, Chardonnay, and Cabernet Sauvignon. Winemakers show increasing interest in exporting their products abroad. Recently, Chile has emerged as a producer of very high quality red wines, usually from a blend of grape varieties.

wine wisdom for one and all

WINE WISDOM FOR ONE AND ALL

Enjoying wine requires little more than common sense—that and the ability to see, smell, and taste.

- Expensive and old don't necessarily mean better.

- It's OK to ask for help when selecting wine.

- With wine especially, variety is the spice of life. Explore different grape varieties from around the globe.

- Taste is personal, so any wine that tastes good to you is a good wine.